DOWN GOSPEL BYWAYS
18 Stories of People Who Met Jesus

Mary Terese Donze, A.S.C.

LIGUORI
PUBLICATIONS

One Liguori Drive
Liguori, Missouri 63057
(314) 464-2500

Imprimi Potest:
John F. Dowd, C.SS.R.
Provincial, St. Louis Province
Redemptorist Fathers

Imprimatur:
Monsignor Edward J. O'Donnell
Vicar General, Archdiocese of St. Louis

ISBN 0-89243-198-9
Library of Congress Catalog Card Number: 83-82582

Cover design by Pam Hummelsheim
Cover photo by H. Armstrong Roberts

Contents

To Joseph —
Prince among men.

To the Reader

Have you ever had this experience? You are driving along a highway, and you see a curious road or a wooded lane and you wish you had time to explore it.

That is what I have done in this book. I have turned aside from the Gospel highways of Matthew, Mark, Luke, and John and have wandered down unfrequented paths. There I came face-to-face with some of the people who move silently in and out of the Gospel stories.

I wondered about these men and women — about their loves, their fears, their aspirations. I wanted to learn more about them, to find out what difference it made in their personal lives to have known and talked to and touched the living Jesus of Nazareth. I spent time with each of them, and from these encounters came *Down Gospel Byways*.

Most of the stories in the book are takeoffs from the Gospel accounts. Some are of episodes the evangelists didn't bother to tell us because they had more important things to say. All of the stories have in them an element of it-might-have-happened-this-way.

I hope that these simple stories will serve as creative aids to those who base their prayer life on the Gospels. All of us, at times, experience periods of dryness when the printed word refuses to yield its riches. At those times, these stories — like the old-fashioned hand pumps that needed to be primed before they gave up their water — may ''prime the spirit'' and open the flow of inspiration to better and higher levels of prayer.

The Author

Now in Jerusalem there was a man named Simeon. He was an upright and devout man. . . . It had been revealed to him by the Holy Spirit that he would not see death until he had set eyes on the Christ of the Lord. Prompted by the Spirit he came to the Temple; and when the parents brought in the child Jesus to do for him what the Law required, he took him into his arms and blessed God; and he said: "Now, Master, you can let your servant go in peace, just as you promised; because my eyes have seen the salvation which you have prepared for all the nations. . . . "

Luke 2:25-31

Simeon

"Grandfather! What are you doing putting on your cloak? I hope you aren't thinking of going out in this weather. You with a cold already."

Miriam lit the little oil lamp on the kitchen shelf. Outside, the cobblestones of Jerusalem were wet with a slow, steady rain, and the winter sky was gray and lowering. The room, too, was damp, and Miriam drew a warm shawl closer about her shoulders. As she spoke to her elderly father-in-law, she took a few dried figs from a wicker basket and placed them before Jeremiah, her six-year-old son, who sat at the small wooden table finishing a bowl of curds.

Grandfather Simeon fumbled with the hook of his cloak. "Now, now, Miriam. It's only a few steps to the Temple."

She shook her head. "You should have gone yesterday when the sun was out and the streets were dry."

Simeon turned toward his daughter-in-law. "Yesterday wasn't the day, Miriam." His voice was gentle.

What he said made no sense to her; but then, he often made no sense. He was a visionary if ever there was one. Forever prating about God's telling him he'd not die before he'd seen the promised Savior. He was looking at her now with that dreamy, faraway look that Miriam had come to accept as part of his approaching senility.

She turned toward the child at the table. "Eat your figs," she said.

"I'm not hungry," the boy replied. "I want to go with Grandfather to the Temple."

"No, you don't!" snapped his mother. "The two of you getting soaked and coming down with colds. Eat your figs." She stooped and put a bundle of sticks onto the small brazier. "The Temple's for men, not for children."

Grandfather cleared his throat. "Miriam, let the lad come. Just this once."

Miriam's face flushed. "Grandfather! You spoil the boy." Her voice was accusing, but she reached over and helped Grandfather Simeon fasten his cloak.

Jeremiah stuffed a fig into his mouth. "If I eat the figs, may I go?"

Miriam threw up her hands. "Go! Go! Both of you. Get sick and who will take care of you?" While she talked, she pulled a long rough scarf from a peg in the wall.

Jeremiah jumped to his feet, stuffing the last of the figs into his mouth.

Miriam tied the scarf about the child's head and shoulders. She poked a finger on each of his bulging cheeks. "Piggy!" she said, but she brushed her lips against his forehead.

It was past time for the evening meal when Simeon and Jeremiah returned from the Temple. The rain had stopped and the sun had come out, but it was low in the sky.

Miriam met them at the door with her brusque grumbling. "There's no depending on menfolk," she said, looking from one to the other. "The soup's been boiling for an hour. Take off your wraps and come eat."

Jeremiah was hungry now and the hot soup smelled good. He sat with his empty bowl before him at the table, waiting for Miriam to fill it and Grandfather Simeon to ask a blessing.

During the meal Jeremiah chattered about the Temple, about the strange robes the priests had worn, the crowds of people, the animals, the birds, the smell of the burning sacrifices. "There was a man and lady there with a baby. Grandfather talked to them and they let him hold the baby. Didn't they, Grandfather?"

Grandfather Simeon smiled and nodded and drank his soup, but he had little to say. Miriam stared hard at him several times during the meal. Something about his eyes disturbed her. They were too bright. He had fever. She should have insisted he stay home that day.

After the evening meal Miriam rolled Jeremiah in his sleeping mat. The boy fell asleep before she finished the kitchen chores.

"Better get yourself to bed, too, Grandfather," she said. "You don't look well. I'll bring you a bowl of hot wine before I go to bed."

Grandfather turned to her when she spoke, but he seemed not to be listening. "I saw the Savior today, Miriam," he said slowly. His eyes burned in his face.

Miriam's lips tightened. It was worse with him than she had thought. He was full of fever, talking out of his head.

She took him by the arm. "Grandfather, go to bed. And stay in tomorrow morning. You're sick."

Grandfather nodded. "You may be right, Miriam. I'll stay in bed."

The sun was well up in the sky the next morning when Miriam went to Grandfather's room. She knocked and walked in. The sunlight streamed through a narrow window. Miriam looked at the old man lying there so peacefully, a smile on his lips. Really, she told herself, he didn't seem that sick after all. Maybe she had been mistaken. She called his name. When he didn't answer, she called again, louder. Suddenly a strange fear took hold of her. She bent and shook the elderly man. He made no response.

Miriam forced herself to keep calm as she walked from the room and went to find her son, who was playing with his pet chicken behind the house.

"Jeremiah!"

The child turned when she called him a second time. He came to her.

Miriam stooped and put her arm about him. "Jeremiah," she asked quietly, "what kind of man and lady was that who talked to Grandfather yesterday?"

Jeremiah shook his head. "I don't know. They just seemed special to Grandfather . . . and he liked the baby. He talked to it as if it were grown up and could understand."

"Ah! The baby! . . . That's it . . . The Savior."

And Miriam wept.

The End

Mary at Easter

The Paschal moon shone through the narrow window in the upper room of the Cenacle and made an oblong of soft light on the worn stone floor near where Mary lay on a low pallet. No one stirred in the house, and, outside, the city was wrapped in silence. Not even a dog bayed. Yet, for all the quiet, Mary was unable to sleep. Yesterday's horrors were still with her. She had dozed a few moments when she first lay down, but now she tossed and turned.

She drew the coverlet closer about her and closed her eyes once more. And there he was, lying limp in a pool of blood at the base of the pillar, the skin of his back hanging in loose strips. She hurried to his side, but a heavy hand held her back, and the soldiers crushed a cluster of thorny brambles on his head. She tried again to reach him where he lay stretched on the wood of the cross, and once more the heavy hand restrained her; and the executioner's hammer lifted, swished through the air, and. . . .

Mary cried out and awoke. Her cheeks were wet with tears. It was no use. Sleep would not come; and, when it did, it was worse than wakefulness. She rose from the pallet and dressed. Through the open window the night air came cool upon her hot cheeks, but deepened her anguish. Its fresh sweetness was fragrant with springtime. Everything outside that window was bursting with new life, blossoming into beauty and loveliness. Yet, how could it be! How could the flowers continue their riot of color or the trees burgeon with blooms when her loved one, her darling, her "lily of the field" hung broken on the stalk, lay trampled in the dust? Yesterday, only yesterday, she had held him in her arms, dead, but still hers. Today. . . .

Mary walked to the window. She looked out over the city where everything lay hushed and in shadow. Beyond the town walls she could make out the crest of Calvary, bleak in the bright moonlight. The crosses had been removed, but in her heart she saw them again, ugly blots against the distant horizon. She closed her eyes as if to erase the picture from her memory and walked back to the low pallet.

For a long time she sat on the side of the small cot, her heart too numb for thought, her lips moving from time to time with his name. "Jesus . . . Jesus."

The hours passed. Toward morning, almost imperceptibly, a healing calm spread over her soul. With the calm came the remembrance of those words he had said so often, "On the third day I shall rise again." After a while, dressed as she was, she once more lay on the cot.

Mary woke with a start and sat up. Someone was in the room. She felt a Presence near her. She stood, and for a moment the breath caught in her throat. There, across the room, standing in the uncertain light of the early morning was Jesus! Her son! Alive!

Mary's arms went out to welcome him. She took a step forward, but the next moment she had dropped to her knees. The Almighty God before her!

At once Jesus was at her side, forestalling her adoration. "Not you, my Mother! Not now!" He lifted her to her feet and folded her in his arms, pressing her to his heart. For a time they stood silent, wrapped in each other's embrace.

Somewhere outside the window a bird burst into song. Mary raised her head and looked into Jesus' eyes. A tear of joy ran down her cheek. He smiled and bent and kissed it away.

Now Mary's hand was on his forehead, parting his hair, feeling the skin. He shook his head and smiled again, knowing her thoughts. She freed herself from his embrace and took both his hands in hers. She turned the palms upward. Her face paled, and tears welled up in her eyes once more. In the center of each palm shone a large irregular gash, healed over, but blood red. She lifted the hands to her lips and kissed the marks.

"It's all right, Mother," he said softly. "They no longer hurt." Once more he drew her to himself and kissed her a second time. Again there was silence between them.

Suddenly, Mary drew away from him. "It is enough, my Son. It is enough. The others . . . they are sorrowing."

"Yes," said Jesus, "they are sorrowing; but they shall see me, and I shall turn their sorrow into joy."

He was gone as quickly as he had come, and Mary stood alone in the room, radiant with happiness.

The End

Now on the way to Jerusalem he travelled along the border between Samaria and Galilee. As he entered one of the villages, ten lepers came to meet him. They stood some way off and called to him, "Jesus! Master! Take pity on us." When he saw them he said, "Go and show yourselves to the priests." Now as they were going away they were cleansed. Finding himself cured, one of them turned back praising God at the top of his voice and threw himself at the feet of Jesus and thanked him. The man was a Samaritan. This made Jesus say, "Were not all ten made clean? The other nine, where are they? It seems that no one has come back to give praise to God, except this foreigner." And he said to the man, "Stand up and go on your way. Your faith has saved you."

Luke 17:11-19

Asa*

The rags covering Asa's leprous feet were tattered and worn, and he trailed strips of the dirty cloth with each step. But it made no difference to Asa. With the three fingers that remained on his right hand, he took firmer hold of his walking stick and plodded on. What matter that the road from Engannim to Jerusalem and the Temple was sixty-five miles. The great prophet from Nazareth had promised sure healing to Asa and his nine companions — all lepers like himself. "Go, show yourselves to the priests," the great miracle worker had said. No more than that. But each man knew in his heart that his cry for help had been heard.

They were on their way now — all ten of them — to the Temple and the priests. They were like boys let out from the synagogue lessons — noisy, shouting for joy, stumbling in their eagerness.

This person is not identified by name in the Gospels.

Only Asa had misgivings. How would he be accepted by the Temple priests? He, a Samaritan. Would they confirm his cure? Or would they refuse to acknowledge his wholeness and condemn him to remain an outcast, even though his body was restored?

Asa's thoughts were interrupted by a shout. "Not that way!" It was Ebenezer, the old leper from Jerusalem, the eldest of their group. Asa had often shared his crusts of bread or his occasional coins with the older man. Ebenezer was pointing to the road leading to the river. "We're crossing the Jordan here," he said. The road he indicated led out of Samaria and across the river into the Decapolis country.

Asa's face showed his surprise. He looked about at the others. The road through Samaria to Jerusalem was more direct, and they knew the countryside well. They had roamed the length and breadth of the land day after day for as long as they had been together. Why take a new and longer route when it was already a four-day trip and wearisome even to a man who was strong and healthy?

Asa opened his mouth to protest the suggestion, then closed it without speaking. His eyes had swept from man to man, and, though no one had spoken, Asa had read the answer to his unspoken protest in their faces. No respectable Jew would walk through Samaritan territory when other roads were open.

It had been different so long as they were lepers and without hope. Then they had been loath to appear in their own neighborhoods, ashamed to be seen by their friends and acquaintances. Now things were going to be different. They were to be free men again.

The group turned and headed toward the river as Ebenezer had suggested. After a moment's awkward silence, following on Asa's silent communication, the men were again in high spirits. But their relationship with Asa had changed.

Each man was suddenly aware of himself as a Jew — and of Asa as a Samaritan.

Their progress was slow, the rotting feet and legs unable to be hurried by the eager spirit. Suddenly, one of the younger men, a mere boy, began to scream. "I'm healed! I'm healed!"

The group stopped and stared at the lad. The boy's disfigured face, his crippled feet, his stubs of arms — all were transformed. He had been made whole.

While they stared — a growing wonder and anticipation on their faces — the man next to Asa let out a shout. "I'm cured! I'm well! Look at me! Look!" But he got no attention. Each man was totally absorbed, finding himself renewed, restored from a living death to full life.

Asa looked quickly to his own hands. Astonishment held him breathless. They were the hands of his early manhood, strong, supple, throbbing with life. At the same time he felt a flow of vitality in his legs and feet. A minute before he had been a leper, a pariah, no better than a corpse. Now he was brimming with vigor, his body clean. And he was free, free to return to his wife and growing son.

Asa's lungs exploded in a cry of exultation. In a frenzy of joy he kicked the rags from his feet, turned from the group, and dashed back along the path they had come. He held his head high, open to the sweep of the wind; and his racing feet puffed clouds of powdery dust from the road.

It was still early afternoon when Asa reached the outskirts of Engannim, where he and his companions had met Jesus less than two hours before. Asa's heart beat with a wild joy at the sight of the town. Engannim! His native town. Before, he had been forced to shun its environs. Now, in less than two weeks he hoped to be back from Jerusalem, free to enter the city and be with his loved ones again. The thought added wings to his feet.

As Asa drew closer to the town, he saw a small cluster of men gathered outside the town gate. From a distance he could make out the Rabbi Jesus among the group.

Asa came shouting and waving his arms. The men with Jesus turned at the noise and backed away from the approaching stranger. But Jesus stepped forward to meet him.

Asa rushed up to Jesus, flung himself on the ground, kissed the rabbi's feet and clung to them with his clean hands.

There was silence in the group. Jesus looked down at the prostrate form before him. Then he spoke, more to himself than to the man at his feet.

"Were not ten made clean? Where are the nine? Is there no one found to return and give thanks but this foreigner?"

Jesus bent and raised the man to his feet. "Your faith has saved you," he said, then added, "Go your way."

Asa had already turned to retrace his steps but stopped short at Jesus' last words. The tone in which they were said surprised Asa into looking back and asking incredulously, "Go *my* way, Rabbi?"

Jesus nodded and a look of understanding passed between them. Minutes later Asa was dashing through the city gates and down the street to home.

The End

. . . Jesus went up to Jerusalem, and in the Temple he found people selling cattle and sheep and pigeons, and the money changers sitting at their counters there. Making a whip out of some cord, he drove them all out of the Temple . . . knocked their tables over. . . .

John 2:13-16

Now when he was . . . by the Mount of Olives . . . he sent two of the disciples, telling them, "Go off to the village opposite, and as you enter it you will find a tethered colt that no one has yet ridden. Untie it and bring it here."

Luke 19:29-30

When he found that Jesus had been condemned, Judas . . . took the thirty silver pieces back. . . . And flinging down the silver pieces in the sanctuary he made off, and went and hanged himself.

Matthew 27:3-5

Judas

Seth took the heavy knotted rope off the peg on the back wall and fingered it carefully. It had the color of bleached bone, but it was as sturdy as on the day he had found it in the outer Temple court three years earlier.

There had been an uproar in the Temple court that day when he had gone to purchase some pigeons for sacrifice. By the time he arrived the fracas had quieted down, but the court was strewn with broken birdcages, overturned tables, and animal dung. Seth had picked his way through the disorder. It was then he had seen the rope. It was lying by one of the Temple columns.

The priests were running here and there, shouting directives and trying to get the court back into order. Seth felt they would be grateful to anyone helping to clean the Temple pavement. So he had picked up the rope.

On his way from the Temple, Seth had passed old Joachim, the beggar, at the Gate. The man had pointed to the heavy knotted rope Seth was carrying and had laughed. "It's done its duty today," old Joachim said. "A young rabbi used it to whip out the hucksters and moneylenders from the Temple court."

Well, that hadn't made the rope any less good, and Seth had brought it home. Today he was glad to have it. After he untied the knots, it would make a stout halter for the new colt he had bought this morning.

"Seth! Seth! Someone's stealing the colt!" Rebekah, Seth's wife, came running into the house from the yard where the colt was tethered to the gatepost.

All morning Seth had been mending a broken plow. He dropped it now, grabbed a strong walking staff from beside the door, and hurried outside.

"Have done with it!" he yelled when he saw two men loosing the colt. He ran toward the gate. "Let be!" he shouted.

Judas, who was one of the men untying the rope from the gatepost, looked up, but he made no move to leave.

Seth glared. The impudence of the fellow!

"Shalom!" called Judas as Seth neared him with the raised staff. "The Rabbi Jesus has need of your beast."

At Judas' words Seth lowered his staff. His face relaxed. So Jesus needed his animal? Well, that was different! If the rabbi wanted to use Seth's colt, all right. Rabbi Jesus could ask anything of Seth. For hadn't the good rabbi cured Seth of his leprosy? Made it possible for him once more to live with his family? To farm his little plot of land?

"Take the animal," said Seth. He loosed the halter and handed the free end of the rope to Judas. "She leads easily."

On the way back to where Jesus waited with a crowd of people, Judas slipped the halter from the colt's neck and slung it across a low branch of an old olive tree. "We don't want this looking like a farm procession or like we're bringing a colt to market," Judas remarked to his partner. "We're leading a King into his kingdom. It should look like it. What we ought to have is a horse, like the Romans."

Half an hour later a happy crowd was moving slowly toward Jerusalem with Jesus seated on the colt. Judas was vigorously waving a palm branch and shouting himself hoarse, "Hosannah!"

There was a metallic clinking of coins hitting, bouncing, rolling on the sanctuary pavement. Judas, throwing down his empty purse, muffled his face with his dark cloak and ran from the Temple. He hurried through the Golden Gate and down the deserted road leading to the Mount of Olives. When he reached the Garden of Gethsemane at the foot of the Mount, he could go no farther. He threw himself on his knees and lay prone across a heavy stone slab. His breath came in short, staccato snorts. For a moment he remained motionless except for his heaving chest. A brisk wind ruffled his black hair.

Suddenly, he let out a low cry, backed from the stone, and stumbled to his feet. He stared at the barren rock. Blood! There on the worn stone were drops of freshly dried blood.

Judas thrust nervous fingers through his hair and looked about. Here at this stone he had found the Rabbi Jesus last night. Now there was blood on the rock. Had Jesus been injured before Judas found him? Been bleeding from some wound? Was this his blood? With a shock of remembrance, Judas recalled the acrid taste in his mouth after he had pressed his lips against the rabbi's cheek.

Judas cursed and flung himself onto the ground. The wind had grown stronger. It cooled his cheek, but it did nothing to soothe his tormented soul. Behind him in the city an innocent man was being condemned to death, and he, Judas, was responsible. He groaned and dug his nails into the sod. From the blackness of his soul came the faintest of whispers, "Friend . . . Friend. . . . "

"Bah!" Judas beat the earth with his fists. "Who would want me for a friend?" The despairing man spoke aloud to the empty garden. "Even *he* could not take me back, forgive me. There's a limit to a man's endurance."

That was it! *There's a limit to a man's endurance.* Judas got to his feet. The sky had darkened, and a gusty wind blew through the olive trees. It was then that he saw it, the rope, the colt's halter, swaying from the branch where he had tossed it last Sunday. Back and forth, back and forth, it swung in the wind.

For a moment, Judas stood mesmerized, his eyes on the moving halter. Then his face hardened with savage determination. He walked to the swinging rope and jerked it from the tree. He looked about. No, not here in the garden. He started for the gate. He had taken but a few steps when a fiery claw ripped open the sky, and a mighty thunderclap rocked the earth. Judas recoiled and lifted a protecting arm before his face. Again the lightning snapped, fierce, terrifying. Judas' nerves gave. He shrieked like a madman, and the wind multiplied the wild echo. Then he dashed headlong down through the Vale of Kidron and on toward the Valley of Hinnom, his dark cloak billowing behind him like an evil specter.

The End

When they reached Capernaum, the collectors of the half-shekel came to Peter and said, "Does your master not pay the half-shekel?" "Oh yes" he replied, and went into the house. But before he could speak, Jesus said, "Simon, what is your opinion? From whom do the kings of the earth take toll or tribute? From their sons or from foreigners?" And when he replied, "From foreigners," Jesus said, "Well then, the sons are exempt. However, so as not to offend these people, go to the lake and cast a hook; take the first fish that bites, open its mouth and there you will find a shekel; take it and give it to them for me and for you."

Matthew 17:24-27

Peter

A trail of broad footprints led down to where Peter had come across the sandy shore to the lake. Now, as he walked through the slush sand where the edge water ebbed and flowed, the imprint of his wide sandals disappeared after each step. He waded into the water, carrying a long fishing pole. He baited the hook and cast the line out into the deeper water. Not since he and Andrew were boys had he gone fishing with an individual line, and the pole in his large hands felt strange and awkward.

While he waited for a nibble, Peter went over the events of the morning. Less than an hour ago the collectors of the Temple tax had stopped him on the street. "Does your master not pay the half shekel?" they had asked.

"Of course he does!" Peter had snapped back. The question had taken him by surprise. Why hadn't they approached Jesus directly? And since every male Israelite over twenty knew his obligation to pay the annual one-half shekel tax, why should they imply that the Master might be remiss?

Later, when he had joined Jesus and his companions in the house, Peter had decided to take up the matter with the Master. But Jesus had anticipated his remarks.

"Peter, do you think the sons of the kingdom should pay taxes?"

"No. Only foreigners."

"Right. But we don't want to scandalize these tax gatherers, so we'll pay the tax."

Peter looked about for Judas, who carried the purse with the general funds.

"No need to take it from the common purse," said Jesus. "Go down to the lake and cast in a line. Take the first fish that bites. In its mouth you'll find a shekel. Give it to the collectors for both of us."

The men with Peter had been talking among themselves. Now, as if by common consent, they fell silent. They looked at Peter, who stood there like a man not sure he heard what he thought he heard. But the next minute Peter had walked out into a small adjoining room. When he came back, he was carrying a long fishing pole. Without looking to right or left, he strode past them and out the door.

Now he was down at the lake, waiting for a fish to bite. He stood quietly, knee-deep in the water; but his mind was seething with questions. If the Master intended to pay the tax, why had he refused to take the money from the general purse? Or, if he meant to furnish the coin miraculously, why hadn't he simply said the word? Wasn't this fish idea a bit foolish? And why was he, Peter, chosen to carry it out?

Peter looked out over the water. The wind was low, and the sea was like a polished mirror. A small fishing craft lay motionless some distance away, its trawl slack in the afternoon sunlight.

Suddenly, Peter's thoughts went back to a night a few months earlier when the Master had asked him to walk on that water. The wind had been high, and the waves wild. How differently he might have performed had the lake been calm like this. Then, almost like a shout, Peter was hearing again the Master's voice that night, "O you of little faith. . . . "

Peter almost dropped his fishing pole. Here was the answer to his questions. The Master was giving him another chance to prove his faith, his trust. Well, he'd try to be equal to it.

At that moment Peter felt a nibble on his line. Instinctively, his rod went up, and a tiny sardine dangled from his hook. Peter made ready to snap the line and free the small fish. No sardine could carry a shekel in its mouth. Too tiny a fish. He'd have to wait for a larger catch, a catfish, a perch. He was ready to let the sardine go when, suddenly, he remembered Jesus' words, "Take the first fish that bites."

For a moment Peter's practical mind struggled with his belief. The next minute he was lifting the pole and swinging the fish toward him. His hands trembled as he grabbed the tiny fish and let the pole slide into the water beside him.

The fish wriggled in his hand. Peter held it firmly. "Lord," he whispered as he looked at the little sardine, "I believe. Help my unbelief." He opened the mouth of the tiny fish. There, upright and seeming to fill not only the mouth but almost the whole quivering body of the little fish, was a shekel, bright, shiny. Peter stared at the silver coin. The old feeling of unworthiness swept over him. "Depart from me, O Lord, for I am a sinful man."

The sardine jerked spasmodically. Peter's hold tightened. He pinched the shekel between his thumb and forefinger and drew it out. Sticking it into the fold of his belt, he carefully removed the hook from the fish's mouth and cast the sardine back into the lake.

Peter stooped for his pole, shouldered it, and waded from the water. Once again his fingers felt for the solid reality of the coin. Then he started up the beach.

Farther along, two fishermen mending their nets raised their eyes momentarily to see a brawny man, striding along, carrying a boy's fishing rod that bobbed up and down on his shoulder, and whistling at the top of his lungs.

The End

One of the Pharisees [Simon] invited him to a meal. When he arrived at the Pharisee's house and took his place at table, a woman came in, who had a bad name in the town. She had heard he was dining with the Pharisee and had brought with her an alabaster jar of ointment. She waited behind him at his feet, weeping, and her tears fell on his feet, and she wiped them away with her hair; then she covered his feet with kisses and anointed them with the ointment.

Luke 7:36-38

Magdalene

Lucius sat on the low cushion beside the couch and let his hand move deliberately up the soft bare arm of the woman who lay there, tantalizingly beautiful in a soft scarlet gown. The next moment, he drew back from a sharp blow in the face.

"Keep your hands to yourself, young peacock." The woman gave a low, mocking laugh.

Lucius, Roman centurion billeted in Capernaum, rubbed his cheek ruefully. "You've a heavy hand, Magdalene. It's half destroyed my intention of telling you about the handsome young rabbi who's in the city today."

"Bah! You and your handsome cubs." Magdalene affected a bored unconcern, and her voice sounded languid when she asked, "Who is he?" But Lucius was not deceived. He slipped from the cushion and knelt by the couch.

"A kiss, my fair one, and the information is yours." He bent to her lips.

Magdalene reached out and pushed his face from her. "Here" — she drew a half-blown rose from her dark hair and bushed it against his lips — "your kiss. Now tell me." And when he came close again — "Away, greedy whelp!"

Lucius laughed, but he backed off. He knew how to bide his time. There would be other days. She was in a restless mood this afternoon. Better to humor her.

"Who is he?" she asked again.

Lucius pretended a sudden preoccupation with the hilt of his short sword and assumed an air of indifference. "On second thought, you probably wouldn't be interested. He's not a woman's man. Travels about with a group of scrubby disciples." Then, to pique her — "A decent Jew for all that, though not exactly the kind to look twice at your type."

Magdalene's dark eyes flashed. She sat up. "Conceited Roman! What do you mean 'my type'? 'wouldn't look twice at me'? He's a man, isn't he?" She stood and drew herself up proudly before him, and there was little of her willowy body that the lines of her soft gown failed to reveal.

Lucius rose, too, and gave her an appraising glance, but she snapped a finger in his face and smiled archly. "I'll wager the kiss you sought that I shall have him at my feet before the week is up. Where is he?"

Lucius roared with laughter. "I accept your wager. He's been preaching down by the lakeside every day."

Still laughing, Lucius turned and started from the room. At the door he turned and looked back. "I'm on my way to see Simon. Send word when I can claim my due."

Lucius had been right. The rabbi was preaching to a group of people when Magdalene reached the lakeside. She took in the gathering with a glance. The crowd was small, not more than fifty she estimated, mostly women, some with small children, others carrying infants. A dozen or more men were in the group. Some were leaning on hoes — apparently laborers from nearby fields or vineyards. Not her type, she told herself, then laughed to find herself repeating Lucius' remark. A few cripples were present, too, their crutches in the grass by their feet. The group was well back from the shoreline, on the slope where the land rose to a grassy meadow. Most sat, but there were some here and there, especially in the rear, who stood.

Magdalene joined these. From her position on the sloping ground she could easily see over the heads of the group to where the rabbi stood on the sandy beach a short distance away. He was young. She guessed him thirty — a little more, a little less. He was of good height, but not tall; not muscular either, but of a supple firmness that lent grace and control to his movements. His black hair, blown by the wind, hung in a loose wave that came to a soft upcurl where it rested on his shoulders.

Handsome, Lucius had said. Magdalene agreed. But there was more to the man — a charm, a presence, a power. Magdalene's pulse quickened. Other men in her life had been easy conquests. Puppets, simpletons, most of them. Or brutes. This man offered a challenge. The thought stimulated her.

She had come to the lakeside wrapped in a long gray cloak. Now she loosened the clasp at her throat and let the garment fall back on her shoulders. Its gray drabness made a striking contrast with the scarlet of her gown. She removed a filmy scarf from her head and pushed her hair back from her face, revealing two great gold ear pendants, gifts of Lucius.

Several minutes passed. Magdalene stood looking at the young rabbi. She feigned an interest in his words but listened to none of them. Somewhere in the crowd a child began to cry. Momentarily, Magdalene's eyes wandered from the face of the speaker. When she turned back, he was looking at her.

At once, everything in her sharpened to attention. She had been waiting for this, counting on it, the moment when he would notice her, become aware of her presence. It would determine her first move. Nothing much. A smile. A stance of the body. Later there would be more.

But his eyes held her. They paralyzed her, rendered her helpless. At the same time, a powerful force seemed to lift her out of herself, away from the crowd, apart. Suddenly, as under a brilliant light, her whole life lay open before her. She looked, fascinated by the sight, unable to turn away. Everything was there: her childhood, girlhood, the years before she began to lend her body to lovers, the woman she was now, her sinfulness, degradation. The shame and horror of it overwhelmed her. Then, just as swiftly and with equal clarity, everything changed, and she saw the woman she might have been. A sob caught in her throat.

It was over in an instant, and she was back at the lakeside, standing in the sunlight with the crowd before her on the grass listening to the young rabbi. But her world had collapsed. She felt weak, dazed. She drew her cloak about her, fastened the clasp with unsteady fingers, and put on her veil. She needed to get away, to be alone, to find herself again. She turned to leave, but stopped short at the sound of the rabbi's voice raised loud and clear.

"Come to me, all you who are weary . . . and you will find rest."

He was speaking to the crowd, to the cripples, the laborers, those burdened with the cares of life. She knew that. But might he not also be speaking to her? Tears sprang to her eyes. She turned and ran up the path and away from the lakeside, her heart delirious with a wild hope.

Simon finished his cup of wine and looked at Lucius. "You won't believe this," he said to the young centurion, "but it was none other than our friend, Magdalene. Came in here two days ago when I had the young Rabbi Jesus to dinner. Knelt at his feet, kissed them, wiped them with her hair; in general, made a fool of herself.''

Lucius nodded. ''I heard about it.'' He emptied his cup and wiped his lips with the back of his hand. Then he laughed uproariously. ''What I'd have given to see her at *his* feet. She planned to have him at *hers* in a week. We had a wager on it.''

''Well, you've won,'' said Simon, ''but from what went on between the two, I doubt you'll be able to collect.''

Lucius shrugged his shoulders and got up from the chair. ''Hmph! No great loss. A woman's a woman. There's still Sarah and Esther.''

Simon laughed and began counting off on his fingers. ''And Adah and Rachel and Susanna. . . . ''

The End

. . . Jesus saw the crowds approaching and said . . . "Where can we buy some bread for these people to eat?" . . . One of his disciples . . . said, "There is a small boy here with five barley loaves. . . ." Then Jesus took the loaves. . . .

John 6:5-11

Joel*

Old Hannah bustled through her daughter-in-law Rebecca's low kitchen door and plopped a wicker basket covered with a clean white cloth onto the table. She kissed Rebecca loudly on the cheek.

"I'm bringing back an exchange for the loaves of bread I borrowed last week," she said. She dropped onto a rough stool by the table and sat fanning herself with her hand. "And I must get your new recipe for bread."

Rebecca scooped the grain she was grinding into a deep wooden bowl and wiped her hands on her apron. She started to speak, but Hannah was talking again. "And for goodness' sake, Rebecca, the next time I need something, don't send Joel. Uncle Simon was going to Capernaum, and I wanted him to take that bread along with him for my brother — the one whose withered arm the great Rabbi Jesus cured — but

This person is not identified by name in the Gospels.

Simon had to leave at three, and it was after four when Joel came trotting in with his basket of bread.''

"Why, that's strange," said Rebecca. "I sent him in plenty of time to get the bread to you before three. And though he's only eight, he ordinarily doesn't dawdle when I send him on errands.''

"Well, he dawdled this time," said Hannah. "Surprised you didn't notice how late he was coming home.''

Rebecca broke one of the loaves and set a mug of cool goat's milk before her mother-in-law. She filled a second cup for herself and sat.

"No, I didn't notice," she said. She brushed a wisp of hair back from her hot cheek. "That was the night the children's father was late coming from the fish market. We waited till he got home and had supper with him, so the boys played in the sheep pasture later than usual. I just supposed Joel had come back and joined them.''

Hannah dipped her bread into the milk and chewed heartily at the dripping sop. A bee droned in through the open window and out the door.

"My own bread isn't too bad, is it?" asked Hannah. She broke off another bit of the loaf.

Rebecca, a morsel in her mouth, shook her head.

"But yours was better," admitted Hannah.

"It's the same as I always make. I don't know why it should taste different.''

There was a scuffle outside. Rebecca looked through the open doorway in time to see her six-year-old son James crying and disappearing around the corner of the house. A minute later, Joel came into the kitchen, his face flushed, his hair rumpled. At the door he turned and yelled back to his smaller brother, "And you keep out of my secret box!''

He turned and saw Hannah. Her presence surprised and confused him.

"I am sorry, Grandmother. I did not know you were here." The small boy bowed respectfully.

Hannah started to speak, but Rebecca interrupted her. They were her boys. She would handle them.

"What are you doing, Joel? Why is your little brother crying?"

Joel's lower lip quivered. "James always messes with my things. He was at my secret box trying to steal my loaf of bread."

Rebecca frowned. "Well, what are you doing with a loaf of bread in your secret box? You don't have to stash away food. There's plenty to eat in the house."

"But this was special bread." There were tears in the child's eyes.

"What's all this fuss about special bread?" Rebecca looked at Hannah. "First you. Now Joel."

Rebecca turned back to her son. "Sit down. I want to know what all this is about."

Hannah tried again to interrupt, but Rebecca ignored her and spoke to Joel. "Now, tell me where you got this special bread that you're hoarding so carefully."

Joel cast a sidelong glance at his Grandmother, who had gotten up to refill her mug. He swallowed a lump in his throat. "You know that bread you had me take to Grandmother?" He kept his voice low.

"Well?"

"A man asked me for it. He had a big bunch of people who hadn't brought their lunch and he wanted to feed them."

"Feed a big crowd with five loaves of bread?" asked Rebecca.

Grandmother had returned with the milk. She heard the child's remark. "The boy is lying," she said.

Rebecca looked questioningly at Joel. "Are you sure, my son?"

The child was silent.

"Well, did you give him your loaves?" Rebecca continued.

Joel nodded.

Hannah broke in. "Rebecca, the boy should be punished. Of course he didn't give the loaves away. He brought them to me."

Rebecca again ignored her mother-in-law's comment, but Joel turned to Hannah. "Grandmother, those weren't mother's loaves. The man gave them to me after everybody had eaten. 'Five of them for your good Grandmother,' he said, 'and one for you.' For me." The tears were back in the child's eyes.

"Who was this man?" asked Grandmother. Her voice had suddenly become gentle.

"I don't know," said Joel. "Everybody just called him Jesus."

The End

As he went along, he saw a man who had been blind from birth. His disciples asked him, "Rabbi, who sinned, this man or his parents, for him to have been born blind?" "Neither he nor his parents sinned," Jesus answered "he was born blind so that the works of God might be displayed in him." . . . Having said this, he spat on the ground, made a paste with the spittle, put this over the eyes of the blind man, and said to him, "Go and wash in the Pool of Siloam" . . . So the blind man went off and washed himself, and came away with his sight restored.

John 9:1-7

Ben-Aser*

Ben-Aser shook the old mat before dropping it at the base of a worn stone column inside the Dung Gate. He pulled his tattered blanket about his shoulders and settled himself for the day's begging.

It was a hard routine for him, this daily trip around the streets of Jerusalem and the long hours of squatting in corners waiting for coins or crusts of bread. But there was no help for it. He had been born blind, and he had no other means of support. His parents were poor; Ben-Aser would not let himself be an added burden to them.

Yes, it was hard, but — thanks be to Yahweh! — he was not helpless. Long ago, Ben-Aser had learned how to get around by himself. There wasn't a street or gate in Jerusalem that was unfamiliar to him. And he had friends — of a sort — people who had seen him begging day after day since he was

*This person is not identified by name in the Gospels.

a lad of ten and had come to know him. Now he was twenty-nine. Often, these friends gave him something. Little enough, to be sure, but something.

Ben-Aser squirmed on his mat and scratched his back vigorously. The fleas were worse here by the Dung Gate, but the sun was warm and the wind not so sharp. When the days grew milder, he would go farther to the north side of the city.

He had just settled himself on his mat when he heard a group of men coming along the street leading to the Gate. Ben-Aser did not recognize the voices, but his hand went out. "A coin, a bit of bread, for the love of Yahweh," he pleaded.

The men had stopped, and at once Ben-Aser realized they were talking about him.

"Rabbi, who has sinned, this man or his parents, that he should be born blind?"

Ben-Aser felt the blood rush to his face. His fists tightened. What dog was this who dared insult his parents? O Yahweh! If only he could see! He'd take on this fellow and thrash him soundly. But blind, what could he do?

In the midst of his angry thoughts, Ben-Aser heard another voice, a calm, strong voice, but gentle, too. "Neither this man has sinned nor his parents. But the works of God were to be made known in him."

A wave of peace passed over Ben-Aser. Who was this unknown friend who was taking his part, speaking for him? Ben-Aser heard the man take a step closer. Then the beggar felt a warm finger spreading something like cool, moist clay over his blind eyes, and the gentle voice was directing him, "Go, wash in the Pool of Siloam."

An hour later the group of men who had spoken to Ben-Aser came back through the Dung Gate into the city.

"Look, Rabbi," said one of them as they passed some

distance from the Pool of Siloam, "the man on whose eyes you put clay is still walking about as if he were blind."

Everyone looked in the direction the speaker was pointing. There was Ben-Aser, his face aglow with happiness, but his eyes closed, walking along the street with the habitually cautious step of someone without sight.

"He sees," said the rabbi.

For a while the group walked on in silence. Then the man who had first questioned the rabbi on Ben-Aser's blindness spoke. "If he sees, Rabbi, why would he close his eyes?"

The rabbi turned to the man who needed to know all the answers and said quietly, "How otherwise is he to find his way home today except he close his eyes?"

The End

And the third day, there was a marriage in Cana of Galilee: and the mother of Jesus was there. And Jesus also was invited, and his disciples, to the marriage. And the wine failing, the mother of Jesus saith to him: They have no wine. And Jesus saith to her: Woman, what is that to me and to thee? my hour is not yet come. His mother saith to the waiters: Whatever he shall say to you, do ye.

John 2:1-5

Mary at Cana

A serving lad came into the kitchen from the small banquet room where Eleazer and Susannah sat with their friends at the wedding feast.

"Lady Mary, we need more wine." The boy flashed her a broad smile and held out the heavy pitcher.

Mary lifted a wineskin from the floor and emptied the remainder of its contents into the vessel. This was the last of the wine, and the worst, too new to be mellow. Three other empty wineskins lay in the corner of the room.

For a moment, after the boy turned away with the pitcher, Mary stood frowning. It was only the fifth day of the wedding celebration and already the wine had given out.

Mary had come to Cana to lend her help to the bridal couple, and she felt a concern now at the failure of wine. What an embarrassment for these two young people if the guests had nothing more to drink. She had thought the supply sufficient, but how could she have guessed that Jesus would bring along six extra guests.

The thought of Jesus brought a smile to her lips. Their mutual presence here was their first meeting since he had left home to begin his public career, and it was good to be together again. She would mention the wine situation to him. He might have a suggestion.

She walked toward the banquet room. From the doorway she caught his eye and beckoned. He rose at once.

"What is it, Mother?" he asked when he stepped into the kitchen. He smiled to see her cheeks flushed and the perspiration on her forehead. The kitchen was hot.

"It's the wine, Jesus. They have no more. I just emptied the last skin."

For a moment, she thought he hadn't heard her. He stood looking directly at her and his smile lingered, but something strange, different, came into his eyes. He reached out and held her at arm's length, searching her face.

"Woman . . . " he said. There was a sudden urgency in his voice. "What is that to you and to me? My hour has not yet come."

His words bewildered her. He had never before spoken to her in this manner. Was he reprimanding her? Telling her she should not have approached him on this matter? No, the tone of his voice denied that. But it was clear that he was trying to tell her something. She read it in his eyes. Everything in her reached and strained and struggled to understand his message.

"Woman. . . . " The word fell strangely on her ear.

Once more her eyes sought his. And, immediately, in some unaccountable way, it was as if she were swept into the distant past, to the dawn of time. She was standing in a garden listening to a promise, "I will put enmity between thee and the woman. . . . "

The woman of prophecy!

Something in Mary's soul broke from its moorings and launched onto a shoreless sea. This man before her was drawing her, lifting her, snatching her up to a new level of being.

But why? What was he asking of her? What did he mean by those strange words: *My hour has not yet come?*

She closed her eyes to listen. Yes, he was speaking to her heart. "Woman" — it was as if she heard his voice speaking aloud — "Woman, you think you are simply asking help with this wine situation. But there is more to your request than you know. The eternal years have waited on this moment. *My* hour has not yet come. But only because *your* hour must precede mine. A woman's word moved our first father Adam to act to mankind's destruction. My heavenly Father desires that another woman's word should release the power within the new Adam unto salvation."

Mary's soul reeled with the thought. Minutes before she had been his mother, asking a simple favor of a dutiful son. Now she was all of humanity, standing at the side of the world's second Adam, with power to help or hinder him by her word. For one sickening moment darkness assailed her soul. "You will be like gods. . . . " Then, through the darkness, she heard again the voice of Jesus, "Woman. . . . "

Mary trembled. She opened her eyes. At the same moment, Jesus released his hold on her arms. It was as if he freed her to do as she willed.

Mary turned. "Come," she called to several of the serving boys who had entered the kitchen. She beckoned them and nodded toward Jesus. "Do whatever he tells you," she said.

The light of heaven shone in Jesus' face. This woman whom God had given him had stood the test. She was using her hour to make his hour possible. She was granting to him as new head of the human race the primacy that was rightly his, restoring to him the power that another woman had usurped in the original plan of salvation.

"Fill the water jars," said Jesus.

His hour had struck, and power went out from him to do her will.

The End

Onica

Sephrona stood by the open window and watched her thirteen-year-old daughter, Onica, and half a dozen other laughing girls disappear down the narrow street to mingle with the crowds milling around in Jerusalem for the Feast of Passover. She sighed and turned to her husband.

"Jairus, I wish you weren't so strict with the girl. This is her first trip to Jerusalem, and tomorrow's the last day of the Feast. Next week we'll be returning to Capernaum. All she and her friends want to do is walk around and look at the booths and bazaars."

Jairus took a small pouch from his wide sash and counted the coins. "I gave her permission, didn't I?"

"After a scene," said his wife.

Jairus returned the pouch to his broad belt. "I don't understand the girl," he grumbled.

Sephrona nodded. "I know. As long as she was an invalid, she was no problem for either of us. Now that the Rabbi Jesus has brought her back to us, alive and well, things are different. She missed out on so much when she was ill. It's as if she were trying to catch up with herself." Sephrona began clearing the few simple utensils from the table where they had eaten their breakfast. "But she's a good girl," she added.

Jairus made no comment. He threw his cloak about his shoulders and left the house.

It was still an hour until noon. Sephrona, stirring the small pot of lentil broth, heard shouts in the distance and glanced out the window. A noisy crowd was passing at the end of the narrow street where it intersected with the thoroughfare leading to the Fortress Antonia. Separated from the crowd and running toward the house was Jairus. Even before he reached the door, Sephrona was there to meet him.

"What is it?" she asked. "What's wrong?" Her eyes searched his face.

Jairus closed the door behind him and looked quickly about.

"Where's Onica?"

Sephrona felt a chill of apprehension. "She isn't home yet. What happened?"

Jairus drew his hand across his sweaty brow. "The Rabbi Jesus has been arrested . . . condemned. They're dragging him to Calvary . . . to execute him. The city's in an uproar. Roman soldiers everywhere."

Sephrona's face went white. She threw a scarf over her head and started for the door.

Jairus caught her by the arm. "Where are you going?"

"To find Onica."

"Are you mad? You'll be trampled in the streets. Leave the girl to me. She should never have gone out."

Jairus walked to the door and stepped out. Sephrona

followed. She looked past him down the street and gave a short cry. Coming toward them was Onica. She was alone and running, her long dark hair streaming in the wind.

Jairus sucked in a quick breath and stared. Impossible! Onica, his own child, grown daughter of the ruler of a synagogue, running through Jerusalem with her head uncovered like a woman of the streets! Men divorced their wives for lesser improprieties. He drew back into the house and slammed the door.

"Lord Yahweh!" he exclaimed. His face was red with anger. "Am I raising a tramp?"

Sephrona trembled, not for herself — she shared his shame — but for the girl.

"Jairus . . . " she ventured.

He ignored her and glanced toward the door, waiting for it to open.

But Sephrona would not be put off. "Jairus, there must be some reason. Let the girl explain when she comes."

Jairus was silent, but his heavy breathing frightened Sephrona. She remained standing close inside the door. If need be, she would protect the girl against her husband's fury.

There was a moment of silence between them. Then, slowly the door opened, and Onica stepped into the room. She closed the door quietly behind her and turned. The girl's face was white, except where a deep crimson spot glowed on each cheek, and her eyes shone with a strange brilliance. She carried her scarf, a tight bundle, rolled in her hands; and the front of her dress was soiled, as if with dirt from the street. She gave a quick glance toward her mother then stood, silent, facing her father.

Jairus strode forward. Sephrona could feel the anger surging through him.

"What do you mean by exposing yourself in public?" he demanded of the girl.

Onica's eyes filled with tears.

"Father . . . " she began.

But Jairus was past listening. "Where is your veil?" he shouted.

The girl held out the rolled scarf.

"It belongs on your head, not in your hands!" Jairus snatched the folded bundle and threw it at her feet. It fell open on the floor.

Sephrona gasped, then dropped to her knees and sobbed aloud, pointing to the fallen scarf. Jairus' eyes went to the floor, and his face blanched. There, imprinted on Onica's soft white veil, was the bloodstained face of the Rabbi Jesus.

The End

One sabbath day he was teaching in one of the synagogues, and a woman was there who for eighteen years had been possessed by a spirit that left her enfeebled; she was bent double and quite unable to stand upright. When Jesus saw her he called her over and said, "Woman, you are rid of your infirmity" and he laid his hands on her. And at once she straightened up, and she glorified God.

Luke 13:10-13

Abigail*

Johanna was sick. There was no doubt about it. Her head hurt and her whole body ached. She rolled over on her mat and called to her six-year-old daughter, sleeping a few feet away.

"Wake up, Rachael."

The child opened her eyes.

"Get up. Put on your clothes. I'm too sick to go with Grandmother to the synagogue this morning. You'll have to take her."

Johanna closed her eyes and tried to sleep.

Rachael hurried into her clothes. She went to wake Grandmother who slept alone in the small room behind the kitchen.

The woman was already up and dressed.

"Shalom, Grandmother," said the child. She walked over and kissed the stooped woman.

This person is not identified by name in the Gospels.

It was easy to kiss Grandmother Abigail. Her body was so bent that her face was almost as low as Rachael's. For eighteen years Abigail had suffered from a spinal disease that bowed her back and made it painful for her to lift her head.

"I'm to take you to the synagogue this morning, Grandmother," said Rachael. "Mother is sick." She prattled on, delighting the older woman.

They were ready to leave. "I don't think you'll need your shawl, Grandmother. The sun's up and shining." Rachael opened the door.

But Grandmother paused and shook a wise finger. "One never knows, little one. It might be chilly in the synagogue. I'd better take it."

The child stepped back from the door and lifted a long, lightly woven scarf from the back of a low chair. She threw it about Abigail's rounded shoulders.

Abigail patted the child's hand. "The Lord bless you, my child."

The walk to the synagogue was short, but they moved slowly. Once before, Abigail had tripped on the front of her skirt and fallen. Her back had been worse after that.

Abigail's skirts were always a problem. Johanna kept shortening them in front and lengthening them in the back as Abigail's spine continued to curve. But the older woman still had to be careful on the uneven cobblestones of the street.

A new rabbi read the Scriptures that morning, someone Abigail had never seen before. She twisted her head to see his face, then settled with Rachael at a place near the door.

At the end of the services, Abigail stopped a friend who had been sitting near and had risen with them to leave. "Who's the young preacher this morning?" she asked.

"The Rabbi Jesus from Nazareth," said the friend.

"He's a man of God," said Abigail.

The friend walked on, and Rachael and Abigail started from the synagogue. They were already some distance down the street when Rachael heard someone calling Abigail's name.

"Grandmother, someone's calling you."

They turned, and Rachael saw the young rabbi standing at the door of the synagogue.

"It's the Rabbi Jesus, Grandmother. He's calling you."

With an effort, Abigail lifted her head slightly and raised her eyes. The youthful preacher was beckoning them. "Come," he called.

The two started back toward the synagogue. "What could he want, child?" Abigail spoke more to herself than to Rachael.

"I don't know, Grandmother. But it can't be something bad. He's smiling."

Most of the congregation from the synagogue had already left, but a few of the men stood around arguing with the young rabbi about Sabbath regulations. When Rachael and Abigail came up the men ignored them, but the Rabbi Jesus came forward and stood before the misshapen woman. He smiled at Rachael and spoke to Abigail.

"I saw you in the synagogue," he said. "You are in pain. How many years have you been like this?"

"Eighteen years — half my life," said Abigail.

"It is enough," said the young rabbi. He reached out and placed his hands on Abigail's head. His touch was as gentle as a woman's.

"Daughter of Abraham," he said, "you are healed of your infirmity."

A strange soothing warmth rushed through every part of Abigail's body. Without any effort, her back slowly straightened, her head came up, and she was once more a whole woman.

It was too much! Too sudden for Abigail. She trembled with joy and amazement. "Praise the Lord!" she exclaimed, and fell to her knees at the rabbi's feet.

Jesus glanced around and saw the men still standing about. Then he turned back to Abigail. He stooped and gently lifted the shawl from Abigail's shoulders.

"You may need this as an apron," he said quietly. He raised her to her feet and pushed the ends of the shawl into her hands, letting his eyes move down the front of her dress.

Abigail followed his glance and gasped. Her skirt, over which she constantly tripped, was up to her knees!

Abigail snatched the shawl from the rabbi's hands and tied the ends quickly about her waist. She looked at him, and her smile lit up his face. Then she grabbed little Rachael's hand and hurried away, a proud new woman, praising the Lord and trailing a length of skirt behind her.

The End

Mark

Mark lay stretched on his back on the flat roof, looking up at the stars that burned low in the hot summer night over Jerusalem. Tomorrow was his birthday; he would be fifteen. But, even better than his birthday, tomorrow Uncle Barnabas from Cyprus was coming to visit.

Mark had not seen Barnabas since Cousin Susannah's wedding at Cana in Galilee three years ago. Mark had gone to the celebration with his father, Zeke, and his mother, Mary. He had been twelve at the time, and Susannah had asked him to be a serving boy for the occasion. Uncle Barnabas had been there, too, but he had stayed only the first few days of the festival. Then he had returned to Cyprus.

Mark knew that Barnabas had heard how the teacher from Nazareth had changed water into wine, water that Mark himself had carried into the house. But Barnabas didn't know what else had happened, and Mark was eager to tell him: when the week's festivities were over, Mark had asked

Cousin Susannah for some of the special wine to take home with him, and Susannah had asked the Lady Mary to give him a small wineskin for his very own.

When he got home, Mark had poured the wine from the skin into a heavy deep jar and had hidden it back in a corner of the cellar where no one ever looked. He meant to save the wine for some important occasion — maybe for his own wedding. Or maybe he'd keep it for his children, even his grandchildren. He'd give them each a sip and tell them the marvelous story of the great Rabbi Jesus and his beautiful mother. Anyway, he'd keep it for something really special. He wasn't sure what. But tomorrow he'd let Uncle Barnabas taste the wine — a small bowl or so — to make up to Barnabas for his having missed the most exciting thing at the wedding.

Mark yawned and rolled over. A few minutes later he was asleep.

Barnabas and Mark had been out, wandering the streets and looking at the sights in Jerusalem all afternoon. Now they were back home and hungry. They stood in the small kitchen, talking and laughing and getting in the way as Mark's mother prepared the evening meal.

Mary put up with them as long as she could. Finally, she waved them out of the kitchen. "Go," she said briskly. "I get nothing done with you two under my feet. Come back after a little. Supper will be ready soon, and Mark's father should be back from the pottery shop any minute."

Mark and Barnabas laughed and left the kitchen. But Mary had scarcely turned again to her cooking when she heard her son calling. He came running back into the kitchen. Barnabas followed and stood just inside the doorway.

"Mother!" said Mark. "Where's my wine jar? My special wine?"

Mary turned from the pot she was stirring and looked at him. "Why, Mark, I wouldn't know. That's been three years. Where did you put it when we came back from the wedding?"

"I had it in a good place . . . where I thought nobody could find it, and it's not there." He had raised his voice, and tears of frustration filled his eyes. He blinked away the tears and bit at his lip.

There was a heavy step at the doorway, and Mark's father came into the kitchen. At once he noticed Barnabas, and for the next few moments the two men exchanged greetings. Then Zeke turned to his wife and son. "What's all this racket about? And why are you raising your voice to your mother, son?"

"Shalom, Zeke," said his wife before Mark could answer. "The boy's not being disrespectful. He's upset about his special wine that he got at Susannah's wedding a few years ago. He can't find it."

"Well, where'd you put it?" asked the older man, turning to his son.

Mark drew the sleeve of his tunic across his face. "I had it back in that corner by the old barrel of broken crocks . . . where that little shelf is."

Zeke stood silent for a moment and frowned in thought. He looked toward his wife and then back at Mark. Slowly, he began nodding his head.

"Mark, I remember that jar. I saw it there when I emptied some cracked pottery into the barrel. I wondered at the time how a wine jar had gotten into that out-of-the-way place."

Mark's face was written over with disappointment. "Father! Didn't you remember it was mine?"

Zeke shook his head. "No, I didn't, son. Maybe I should have, but I didn't. I just thought it must be a jar I had put there so long ago that I had forgotten about it."

Mark's lower lip quivered. He was fifteen, a man, but this was just too much. His precious wine gone! The best thing he'd ever owned. Something nobody else had. Something from the good and wonderful Lord Jesus himself. And it could never be replaced. Mark was miserable. He looked at his father.

"You didn't drink it, did you, Father?"

"No, I didn't drink it," said Zeke. "I just tasted it and thought, 'This excellent wine must be kept for a special occasion.' "

For a moment Mark's face brightened. So the wine was still around. Father had only moved it to a different spot in the cellar.

But Zeke went on. "I put it back in the corner where I found it," he said. "But at last Passover time, when the Rabbi Jesus honored my home and family by asking to use our upstairs room for the Passover meal, I wanted to give him the best of everything he needed. So I offered him that wine."

Zeke looked about at them all. "And each of us here knows what he did with it," he said quietly. He paused and in the silence that followed, he studied the face of the boy before him. In an instant it had become transformed. Gone were the distress and unhappiness. Joy and wonder filled the boy's eyes — and pride, a surpassing pride.

Zeke smiled and put his hand on Mark's shoulder. "That's where your wine went, son."

The End

. . . Jesus showed himself again to the disciples . . . by the Sea of Tiberias. . . . Jesus called out, "Have you caught anything, friends?" And when they answered "No," he said, "Throw the net out to starboard. . . ." So they dropped the net, and there were so many fish. . . . one hundred and fifty-three of them. . . . Jesus said to them, "Come and have breakfast. . . ." After the meal Jesus said to Simon Peter, "Simon son of John, do you love me . . .?"

John 21:1-15

"Simon, Son of John"

"Hal-loo-o-o-o!"

Simon Peter, Thomas called the Twin, Nathanael from Cana in Galilee, the sons of Zebedee, and the two others in the boat peered through the early morning mist.

"Someone calling over there," said Thomas. He pointed to the shore where they had left their casks and baskets. Through the haze the men could make out the dim figure of someone standing at the water's edge.

"Friends, do you have any fish?" The Stranger's voice rang clear over the water.

"No!" shouted Peter.

"Cast your net to the starboard," called the Stranger.

The night had been long, the men had nothing to show for their labors, and they were tired. A catch at this hour of the morning was unlikely. Yet, there was something authoritative in the Stranger's voice, something more of command than suggestion. They looked at Peter.

"Throw in the net," Peter said.

The men swung the net over the side of the boat. It scarcely had time to sink when there was a pull on the ropes, and the small boat rocked.

"Snagged!" said Nathanael, bracing himself with his foot against the side of the boat and pulling hard on the cordage he held.

But Peter's experienced eye caught a flash of silvery motion just below the surface of the water.

"Fish!" The word exploded on his lips.

For the next few minutes the men struggled with the net.

"Hold it!" ordered Peter. "We'll have to drag it. The boat's too. . . . "

"It's the Lord!" interrupted John.

Peter stopped midway with his directions to the men, his mouth open. He looked at John. The Lord? Of course. *Of course!* How else account for this catch when all the odds were against them?

Immediately, Peter was over the side of the boat and swimming toward the shore.

The seven of them lay on the sand, filled with the bread and fish the Stranger had prepared for them and speaking happily with him, for John had been right. It was the Lord. The men's fatigue was forgotten in their joy at this unexpected appearance of the Master. They lay stretched out, relaxing, content with this most happy turn of events.

There was a lull in the talk, and Jesus rose from where he sat on the sand. He turned toward Peter and asked abruptly.

"Simon, son of John, do you love me more than these?"

It was a strange personal question. The men were taken by surprise. Peter became flustered. He sat up. He looked at Jesus and then at the group. Love the Master more than these other men loved him? How could he say? Over there lay John, who had remained faithful through those difficult Passover days, had stood beneath the Master's cross until the end. Peter couldn't compare himself with him. And Nathanael? By Jesus' own avowal he was an "Israelite without guile." Peter thought of the others. He couldn't compare himself with any of them. He didn't know. All he could answer was about the feelings of his own heart. Of these he was sure.

"Lord," he said, "you know that I love you." His tone was confident.

The men, sensing a change in the casual talk, sat up one by one.

"Feed my lambs," said Jesus. He kept his eyes fixed on Peter.

Peter looked inquiringly at the Lord, but the expression on Jesus' face remained unchanged, and the Master asked once more, "Simon, son of John, do you love me?"

Peter was taken aback. He stood, frowning in thought, his fingers intertwined in his belt. Did the Master doubt his love? Peter puzzled within himself. He was rash. He knew that. Impetuous. Always jumping headlong into situations and decisions where more prudent men held off. Loudmouthed, too, and full of hot impatience. But love the Master? With all his heart!

"Yes, Lord," Peter declared ardently. "You know I love you."

Jesus answered in the same even tone, "Feed my lambs."

The other men were rising now, and they walked silently to the boat a few paces away, drawing the net of fishes farther up on the beach and beginning to put the catch into the casks and baskets. Several of them counted the fish aloud, "One, two, three. . . ."

"Simon, son of John . . . " Jesus began again.

56

The men went on counting. "Eleven, twelve, thirteen, fourteen. . . . " They felt awkward and uncomfortable hearing Peter addressed for the third time.

"Simon . . . do you love me?"

Peter was saddened. The Master asking for the third time whether he loved him! He was hurt, but he had it coming to him, Peter told himself. He deserved it. Hadn't he denied the Master three times? What could he do now? Protest his love? He had done that with oaths the night before he betrayed his Lord.

The brawny fisherman felt confused. He thought he knew he loved. Maybe he didn't. Maybe he was a fraud, a sham. He was no longer sure of himself. He looked at Jesus. Only the Master could save him, could make real the love he thought he had in his heart. Peter cleared his throat. "Lord," he said, "you know all things. You know that I love you."

"Feed my sheep, Peter."

For the next few moments Peter had nothing to say, but a flash of understanding had broken over him and his silence was filled with gratitude. The Master had once again appointed him head of his flock, had vindicated his position before the others, had assured him that his denials had made no difference in their relationship.

In the silence, Jesus went on. "I tell you, Peter, when you were young, you girded yourself and walked where you pleased. But when you are old, you will stretch out your hands, and another will gird you and lead you where you would rather not go."

In a flash the future opened then closed for Peter. It was too much for him. The divine had come too close. He felt disoriented, treading on alien territory. His mind groped for the familiar, for the reality of the commonplace. He turned to the men counting the fish. Could not they at least be with him in what was to come?

"What of that man, Lord?" Peter indicated John.

"I have my own plans for him," said Jesus. "You . . . you take care of Peter. See that you follow me."

There was a rebuke in the words, but the tone was affirming. Peter turned back to Jesus. Their eyes met, and Peter suddenly laughed — at himself. Jesus nodded approval.

The men looked up, relieved. The tension had broken. But, immediately, Jesus was gone and they were alone, the seven of them with the fish.

"How many?" asked Peter, surveying the casks and baskets.

"One hundred fifty-one . . . fifty-two . . . fifty-three!" finished James, as he dropped a perch and two catfish into separate casks.

The End

He entered Jericho and was going through the town when a man whose name was Zacchaeus made his appearance; he was one of the senior tax collectors. . . . He was anxious to see . . . Jesus . . . but he was too short . . . so he . . . climbed a sycamore tree to catch a glimpse of Jesus. . . . Jesus . . . spoke to him: "Zacchaeus, come down. . . . I must stay at your house today.". . . he hurried down and welcomed him joyfully. They all complained when they saw what was happening. . . . And Jesus said . . . "Today salvation has come to this house, because this man too is a son of Abraham; for the Son of Man has come to seek out and save what was lost."   Luke 19:1-10

Zacchaeus

Zacchaeus, senior tax gatherer at the Jericho house of tribute, twined his stubby legs about the legs of the tall stool in the tax booth. He anchored his elbows on the high counter and, settling his chin in his cupped hands, stared absently out into the afternoon sunlight. He was tired but content. It had been a profitable day, and his deep pockets carried a sizable sum of personal profit. In an hour he would close shop.

The booth was hot. The sun beat down on the low roof, and its glare from the cobblestoned street was harsh on Zacchaeus' eyes. A few people milled about the booth, but they were intent on their own concerns which had nothing to do with him.

For a while, Zacchaeus' eyelids drooped. Later he would swear he hadn't dozed, but when a commotion started outside the booth his head went up with a sudden jerk.

A crowd was coming up the street. People were talking excitedly, some running ahead, others drawing to the side as if waiting for whoever was still to pass.

"What's going on?" Zacchaeus called from where he sat in the booth.

A lame beggar, who was hobbling to get ahead before the crowd closed in on him, shouted back but kept on his way.

"The rabbi from Nazareth has come to town."

Zacchaeus was off his stool in an instant. The rabbi in town? The man everyone from Galilee to Jerusalem was talking about? The miracle worker? Zacchaeus lowered the wooden frame that closed the counter for the night. He pushed his account books into a low drawer, locked the door, and came out into the street to join the crowd.

He pushed himself into the thick of the group, using his elbows and shoulders to work his way ahead, determined to see the famed young rabbi. Rumor even had it that a former tax collector was among his intimate followers.

Zacchaeus chuckled at the idea of a tax gatherer turned preacher. The man had to be a fool to exchange the security of padded pockets for a life of tramping about the country-side with an itinerant rabbi and living a hand-to-mouth existence.

Zacchaeus kept moving, but the crowd was slow. With his own short stature and the human wall between him and the rabbi, he was getting nowhere. He was hot, too. Miserably. Suddenly, he stopped, and his face brightened with an idea. The next moment, he had broken from the crowd, gone off to the side of the street where there were few people, and was hurrying ahead of the group. As he ran, he pulled his tunic above his knees and caught the surplus length with his belt. A good distance ahead of the crowd he stopped, circled his arms about an old sycamore by the side of the street, and pulled himself up into the tree. As soon as he got his feet into a convenient crotch, he sat and edged himself carefully out on a stout limb. He swore colorfully at a short stiff twig that tore a strip of skin from his leg, but the pain was only a thing of the moment, nothing to bother about.

Once settled, Zacchaeus looked down toward the crowd coming his way and grinned with satisfaction. His efforts had paid off. Already he could see the sun-tanned face of the man who was the focus of attention.

The crowd came nearer. Zacchaeus kept his eyes fastened on the young preacher. Something about the earnest, open expression on the rabbi's face awakened in Zacchaeus a depth of emotion. It was as if he saw himself again a youth, full of noble aspirations, eager to make something worthwhile of his life. The thought of what he was now and what he had hoped to be hurt Zacchaeus like the opening of an old wound. Suddenly, he found himself wishing he knew the man coming his way, could speak with him, be his friend. Just as swiftly, he grimaced at the idea of his expecting friendship with one whose values in life must be so different from his own.

Zacchaeus inched farther out on the limb and pushed aside a leafy bough. Now the man was almost directly beneath him. Zacchaeus stared in frank admiration.

"Zacchaeus!"

The man in the tree jerked and half lost his balance. The rabbi was calling him by name! The young preacher had stopped and was looking up into the tree.

The crowd had stopped, too, and all eyes were on Zacchaeus. People poked one another and pointed and burst into laughter. At another time his ludicrous position would have embarrassed Zacchaeus. He, a grown man, chief tax collector of the city, up a tree, his tunic above his knees, his short bare legs straddling a limb, and his sandals dangling over the heads of the passersby.

But the fool he looked never entered Zacchaeus' mind. He had heard the rabbi calling his name. He trembled with astonishment and joy.

And now the rabbi was speaking again.

"Zacchaeus, come down. . . . I must stay at your house today."

Incredible! The great wonder-worker wanting to be his guest! Zacchaeus swung one leg over the branch, let himself hang by his hands, and then dropped to the ground.

The crowd stood watching as the rabbi, his band of twelve, and the runty tax gatherer disappeared up the street. The simply curious in the group laughed, turned about, and went home. The self-righteous, who felt they had been cheated, sought each other out and stood around for the next hour, indignant, scandalized, and carping about the impropriety of the rabbi's action.

And all the while, inside a house up the street, a lost son of Abraham was drinking wine and making merry with the Son of God and being won to salvation.

The End

. . . Jesus . . . sat . . . by the well. . . . When a Samaritan woman came to draw water, Jesus said to her, "Give me a drink." . . . The Samaritan woman said to him, " . . . You are a Jew and you ask me, a Samaritan, for a drink?" . . . "If you only knew what God is offering . . . you would have been the one to ask, and he would have given you living water." . . . "Sir" . . . "give me some of that water. . . ." The woman . . . hurried back to the town . . . "Come and see a man who has told me everything I ever did; I wonder if he is the Christ?" . . . the Samaritans came up to him, they begged him to stay with them. . . . "Now we no longer believe because of . . . you . . . we have heard him ourselves and we know that he really is the saviour. . . . "

John 4:6-42

Leah*

Leah's shapely hips swung with her rhythmic stride as she balanced the empty water jug on her head and carried a small pail at her side. She was on her way to Jacob's well on the outskirts of the city. The midday sun was overhead, and she had the path to herself. There were cooler hours for fetching water, but none like this when she could be alone.

Not that Leah preferred the solitary trip. She had a woman's natural liking for talk and companionship, but the maids and matrons of Samaria had long avoided her, ignored her.

The women had their reasons. For one thing, Leah kept an inn and mixed with all types of people who patronized it. Also — and it was common knowledge — she was an adulteress.

*This person is not identified by name in the Gospels.

63

At first Leah had suffered from the women's unfriendliness; then she had hardened herself against it and become bitter; now she didn't care, she told herself.

Once outside the city gate, Leah hummed a bright, rollicking tune that gave an even swing to her steps and helped keep her mind from the noon heat. Suddenly, she stopped humming. From a distance she saw someone sitting by the side of the well on the stone ledge under the great oak. A little farther along she made out the stranger to be a man. A Jew. She could tell from his clothes.

Leah was hot and sweaty when she reached the shade of the oak. Without glancing at the stranger, who sat less than ten feet from where she stood, Leah took the jar from her head, removed the wooden cover from the well top, and began to lower the pail, playing out the rope through her cupped hands. In a matter of minutes she had drawn the vessel back to the rim of the well and was emptying the water into her jar.

"Give me a drink." It was the stranger speaking.

Leah started at the sound of his voice, and some of the water from the pail ran down the side of the jar to the ground. She set the pail on the edge of the well and turned to see the man reaching out a small cup.

He was young, maybe thirty, her own age, and he looked directly at her in a frank, friendly way. Immediately, she felt at ease in his presence, as one feels with a favorite brother. It was a new experience for her — to react this way with a stranger, a man. But she would be wary. She took the cup, filled it, and handed it back.

"You're a Jew," she said. She watched him drink. "Why did you ask me for water? You know I'm a Samaritan."

The stranger ignored the question.

"If you knew me," he said, "maybe you'd ask me for a drink, and I'd give you living water."

Living water? Was he making sport of her? She looked about. "You don't have a bucket or a jar," she said, "and the well's deep. Where would you get living water? Do you consider yourself greater than our father, Jacob, who gave us this well?"

If the stranger recognized the barb in her words, he gave no indication. He pointed to the water in her jar. "Anyone who drinks of this water will get thirsty again. The water that I give will be like an inner fountain that forever satisfies one's thirst."

Leah thought of her many trips to the well. "Give me this water, Sir, so I needn't make these daily trips in the heat."

"Go first and call your husband and come back."

Leah stooped and lifted the wooden cover to replace it on the well. She avoided the man's eyes.

"I have no husband," she said. She hated herself for the lie. The man before her deserved better. He had been decent to her.

"You're a truthful woman," said the stranger. "Someone less honest would not have admitted to living with a man not her husband."

For the moment, Leah was speechless. Who was this man? She had lied to him, and somehow he had seen through her deceit. Nevertheless, instead of despising her, he had deliberately given her lying words an honorable interpretation, made them a matter of praise.

"Sir, I perceive that you are a prophet," Leah remarked and abruptly steered the conversation along other lines. "We Samaritans and you Jews worship at different places. Which is the right location?"

"The place doesn't matter," said the stranger. "True worship is in the heart."

"I think that when the Messiah comes," said Leah, "he'll answer such questions for us and tell us many things."

The stranger smiled. "Yes," he said, "he's telling you some of those things now. Spread the Good News."

Half the water in her jar spilled along the path, and Leah's hair and shoulders were dripping when she stepped into the inn courtyard where the men gathered each afternoon for the local news. A group of them were there now, talking and drinking the inn's weak wine. They greeted Leah. Hers was the most frequented inn in the locality, and the men liked her. They liked her service, her style — another reason for the womenfolk's antagonism.

From the group, a burly merchant, a frequent patron at the inn, called out to her. "You've had something stronger than this wine, Leah, that you couldn't get home without spilling the water." He laughed good-naturedly.

On another occasion, Leah would have met his bantering remark with an equally waggish reply. Today she ignored it, set down the water jug, and looked around. Most of the faces were familiar. Good. She was among friends with whom she could share the great news that she had seen and spoken with the Messiah.

But she would choose her words carefully. Not a man in the group would be beholden to a woman for even such information as she had to share. She must make it appear that she was deferring to their judgment rather than informing them. She frowned in thought.

The brawny merchant moved up beside her. "What's doing, Leah?" He chucked her under the chin with the familiarity of an old friendship.

Leah brushed away his hand. "I just came from the well," she said. "There's a man there who told me everything I ever did."

The merchant threw up his hands in mock amazement, and the men laughed loudly.

66

But Leah would not be turned from her purpose. The laughing stopped, and the men waited to hear more. Leah knew it was important now that she play her part prudently.

"I don't know . . . " she began, then paused. "I wonder . . . Could such a man be the Messiah?"

The ruse worked. She went about her business, but she knew she had stimulated their curiosity.

The following afternoon, when the men gathered in the courtyard and Leah came with the wine, the lusty merchant turned to her.

"Remember the man you talked about yesterday?"

Leah wanted to shout, to say she'd never forget him, his kindness, his warmth, his goodness to her, but she merely nodded.

"Well, we went to see for ourselves, and we found out he's the Messiah. We'd never have picked that up from what you said. What's more, he's agreed to spend a few days among us. You think you could put him up here at the inn?"

Leah pretended to think for a moment. It would not do to seem too eager.

"I believe there's an empty room or two in the rear," she said. She kept her voice casual, but her heart sang. She'd give him the best room in the house!

The End

*. . . a man with an unclean spirit. . . . lived in the tombs . . . .
Jesus [said] . . . "Come out of the man, unclean spirit." . . . the
unclean spirits begged him, "Send us to the pigs, let us go into
them." So he gave them leave. With that, the unclean spirits came
out and went into the pigs, and the herd of about two thousand pigs
charged down the cliff into the lake, and there they were drowned.
. . . the people came to see what had really happened. They came
to Jesus and saw the demoniac sitting there, clothed and in his full
senses . . . and they were afraid. . . . Then they began to implore
Jesus to leave the neighbourhood.*

Mark 5:1-17

Eben *

It was still dark when Lemuel's mother, Johannah, wakened
him, but this getting up before daylight was part of their daily
routine. Lemuel had to get to his work. From mid-June until
early September, and from dawn to dusk, he helped watch
over a townsman's great herd of swine that rooted and fed in
the pastureland high on the eastern ridge above the Sea of
Galilee.

Now the boy sat before his breakfast of barley bread and
goat's milk, before taking off for the hills. His mother shared
the meager meal.

"Did you see your father yesterday?" she asked.

Lemuel had just filled his mouth with a chunk of bread. He
nodded.

This person is not identified by name in the Gospels.

"How is he?" asked Johannah.

Lemuel avoided her eyes and shrugged diffidently.

This, too, was a daily ritual with them — Johannah asking about the boy's father, always the same question, and Lemuel making the same wordless response. It was a painful moment for both of them, but Johannah never omitted it.

Three years ago, Eben, the boy's father, had taken ill with a strange malady. It left him bereft of his wits. He became so violent that it was no longer safe to have him at home. The village authorities took over and tried to restrain him with chains, but Eben broke every shackle. Now he roamed the open country, living mainly among the tombs. He seemed more a beast than a man, his hair long and dirty, his beard straggly and matted. Often he was naked, having torn off any clothing he may have had.

Several times a week Johannah sent Lemuel with a wicker basket filled with food, doing without food herself that she might have more for him, and at rare intervals she sent along clothing. On his way to the hills Lemuel would leave the food and clothing on a large flat stone where he knew his father would see it, and then the boy would run away before Eben appeared.

From the hill where Lemuel herded the swine, he could look down to the place of the sepulchers. Occasionally, he caught a glimpse of his father moving wildly among the tombs or heard him screaming and saw him cutting himself with sharp stones. The sight sickened Lemuel. He watched only because Johannah had asked it of him, but it tore at the boy. Had his father died three years ago, when he first took ill, the wound would have been healed by now. As it was, to witness this living death of someone he loved was almost more than the young man could handle.

Lemuel turned and started for the door. He picked up the basket of food for Eben.

"Take this, too," said Johannah. She handed him a small bundle. In it were the last of Eben's clothes, his Sabbath tunic and cloak.

It was afternoon now. Johannah sat on the floor, grinding barley. Suddenly, she stopped, listened, frowned, and listened again. The voice outside was Lemuel's. But what was the boy doing back home at two in the afternoon?

She rose and walked toward the door, but it flew open and Lemuel dashed in. His face was flushed and his breath came in short gasps, as if he had run all the way from the hills.

"Mother! The pigs! They're dead! Drowned!"

Johannah looked at the wild-eyed boy. Then she took hold of him and shook him by the arms. "Get your breath and talk sense. Pigs drowned? On a hilltop? What's the matter with you?" Was the boy taking ill with the same madness that had settled on his father?

Before Lemuel could answer, there was a screaming and laughing outside the house, and a stream of people ran past the door.

Lemuel started back out, but Johannah shoved the door shut and pushed him onto a chair. "You stay right here until I know why you're not where you belong!" Her anxiety had unnerved her and her voice was shrill.

Lemuel slumped on the chair. He breathed heavily for several minutes before speaking. "I was with the pigs," he began, "and all at once the air on the hill got hot . . . like an oven . . . quickly . . . just like that!" He brought his hands together with a resounding bang. "Every pig stopped rooting, its head went up, its ears lifted, its bristles stuck out. The next minute the whole herd took off, squealing like demons, and flew out over the cliff side of the hill into the sea." Lemuel gasped for breath. "All two thousand. The sea's full of them."

The noise outside grew louder. Lemuel left the chair. "It's the people," he said. "They're going to see the pigs." He moved toward the door. "I want to go along."

Johannah made no attempt to stop him now, and the next minute he was out of the house. She shook her head and watched him run down the street. For a while, she stood by the window. When the noise let up, she went back to grinding the barley.

Johannah's relief at knowing the boy was not ill brought her peace, but if the pig situation was as he said, he no longer had a job. How would they manage? His earnings had been a mere pittance, but they had eked out a livelihood on it. The future? . . .

The street was quiet now, and inside the house the only sound was the cracking and crunching of the barley beads under the grindstone. A few minutes more and Johannah would have tomorrow's measure of flour ready for the bread.

The door opened. Johannah heard it above the noise of the grinding. Without turning she asked quietly, "Back so soon?"

"After three years this does not seem soon," a voice answered.

Johannah stopped grinding the barley. The voice was Eben's, the same voice she had heard so often during these three years when she dreamed he was back with them, entering the kitchen in his old familiar way. But always she had known she was dreaming. Now it seemed real. Johannah shook her head. She chided herself. It had been a long time since she had felt so little control over her feelings. She was overwrought, she told herself. The boy Lemuel had upset her. She continued grinding the barley.

"Do you not wish to welcome me?" the voice went on.

Johannah dropped the grinding stone. She sprang to her feet and turned toward the doorway. For a moment she felt the blood drain from her face. Her knees trembled. She opened her mouth to speak, but no words came. Yet, if it was a vision, oh, what a blessed vision! There stood Eben, more real than she had ever seen him in all her imaginings, dressed in the Sabbath clothes she had sent with Lemuel this morning. She tried again to speak, but now it was impossible because someone's lips were on hers and two strong arms held her close.

For days after that, Eben had to repeat over and over what had happened. "His name was Jesus, and he drove a legion of demons from my soul and body and sent them into the swine."

The common folk could not hear the story often enough, and their hearts warmed toward the compassionate stranger who had brought Eben back to them healed and whole. "We would know more about this man," they said.

But the village officials felt threatened. A man with all that power? He could ruin them. "He's dangerous," they said. "We've asked him not to return." They were afraid of dangerous men.

The End

. . . before they [Mary and Joseph] came to live together she was found to be with child. . . . Her husband Joseph, being a man of honour and wanting to spare her publicity, decided to divorce her informally. . . . when the angel of the Lord appeared to him in a dream and said, "Joseph son of David, do not be afraid to take Mary home as your wife, because she has conceived what is in her by the Holy Spirit."

Matthew 1:18-20

Joseph

Old Ezra pushed open the door to the carpenter shop and greeted the young man behind the workbench.

"Shalom, Joseph Bar-Jacob."

Joseph, the village carpenter, rose from the stool where he sat smoothing the handle of a new scythe and came forward. Tall, with dark eyes and darker hair, Joseph moved with a quiet, easy grace.

"Shalom, Ezra. What can I do for you?" His voice was warm and friendly.

Ezra placed a broken distaff on top of the workbench. "Dinah, the wife, needs a new distaff. She wants. . . . " He stopped. Before him on the workbench, printed in a thin layer of sawdust, was a girl's name: M A R Y. Ezra grinned, glanced at Joseph and back to the workbench.

The young carpenter let his eyes follow Ezra's and flushed like a small boy caught in some minor mischief. Then he laughed good-naturedly and moved his broad strong hand gently over the mound of dust, wiping out the name.

"You miss your little lady, eh?" Ezra's smile was paternal.

Joseph nodded. Everyone in Nazareth knew that he was engaged to Mary, ward of the priest Zechariah.

"Fine woman!" said Ezra.

When Ezra finished with his business and left, Joseph went on with the scythe. He whistled as he worked. Three months ago, in early April, his fiancée had gone to visit her cousin Elizabeth at Ain-karim, a small town southwest of Jerusalem. She was returning tomorrow. Joseph's heart was light.

Joseph sat in the room behind the carpenter shop, his face in his hands. It was evening, and the light from a sputtering candle threw grotesque shadows on the wall behind him. Before him on the table lay a half-eaten broiled fish and a broken loaf of bread. A dish of figs stood untouched.

Two months ago Mary had returned from her stay with her cousin. She and Joseph had met since then and had renewed their promises of fidelity. Custom limited further visits, and he had to be satisfied with an occasional sight of her passing the carpenter shop with the other women on her way to the village well.

The days passed routinely for both of them; but, as the months moved into summer, Joseph began to puzzle over a change in Mary. It was hard to say what had changed, but she was different. More beautiful, to be sure, but something else. Then he learned the awful truth. She was pregnant!

Had the child been his, all would have been well. The Jewish solemn engagement was almost as binding as the marriage contract. While it was not common for engaged couples to anticipate conjugal rights, a conception during the time of betrothal was not frowned upon. But the child that Mary carried in her womb was not of his seed.

He sat in the silence of the half-dark room and recalled how, at first, he had not allowed himself to believe this had happened to Mary, to him. But when the evidence forced itself upon him, when friends who came into the shop began to congratulate him, he knew he could no longer keep up the pretense.

Tonight he must decide on a course of action. The law offered him the choice of publicly renouncing Mary or of putting her away privately. Either alternative was odious to him. His heart would not let him believe she had been unfaithful. There had to be some awful mistake. Every moment he had spent with this woman, every thought he had ever entertained of her, each word she had spoken to him had been a benediction on his soul, had made him a better, purer man. Now this horrible thing had come between them.

Joseph lowered his head to the table. He tried to pray. But how does a man pray to undo a fact. He groaned. "Yahweh! Have pity on me!" A sob escaped him and for a while he wept bitterly, then prayed and wept again.

It was late when he blew out the candle, but he had made his decision. He would put Mary away privately. There was nothing else to do, for her, for himself. But it shattered his hopes for the future. Had she died, his heart could not have been more torn. He rose from the table and threw himself onto his mat for the night.

"Joseph! Son of David! Do not fear to take Mary, your wife, for that which is begotten in her is of the Holy Spirit. She shall bring forth a son, and you shall call his name Jesus, for he shall save his people from their sins." The vision faded.

Joseph stirred in his sleep. His eyelids fluttered. Suddenly, he jerked awake and sat up, half dazed. " . . . begotten of the Holy Spirit . . . shall save his people. . . . "

The next minute he was wide-awake. He sprang to his feet, breathless with his new knowledge. Mary, his beloved, carrying the long-expected Savior! Oh, the incredible goodness and mercy of Yahweh!

Joseph flung out his arms in the darkness, threw back his head, and his spirit soared. "God, be praised! O God, be praised!" His voice, his whole being quivered. Dropping to his knees, he lay prostrate on the floor, lost in a wordless adoration and wonder.

He was in the shop before sunrise, sitting at the workbench, humming bits of psalms, and sketching at the design of a headpiece for an infant's cradle.

The End

As they were leading him away they seized on a man, Simon from Cyrene, who was coming in from the country, and made him shoulder the cross and carry it behind Jesus.

Luke 23:26

Simon of Cyrene

A rough hand grabbed the neck of Simon's stout tunic, and he was pushed forward through the screaming crowd that surged along the streets leading from the Fortress Antonia.

"You! Here!" yelled the Roman soldier who had collared Simon and was shouting over the noise of the crowd. "Get yourself in there and carry that wood."

Before he had time to resist, Simon found himself thrust between a mass of pushing, jostling bodies and thrown into the path of a man stumbling along under the weight of a heavy wooden cross.

"Take hold!" ordered the Roman.

Simon had recovered his wits by now. He turned on the Roman, but a leather lash cut across his face and sent him reeling against the man who staggered along under the cross. Simon kept his footing, but the condemned man fell to the ground and lay with the heavy wood on his fallen body.

"Up! Up with it!" shouted the Roman.

Simon seethed with anger, but he lifted the cross and shouldered it. At the same time the Roman pulled the prisoner to his feet. They moved forward, pressed by the noisy crowd. Several times along the way the Roman used his whip to keep the mob from crushing the condemned man.

By now they had passed through the Fish Gate and were on the open road to the mount of execution. Simon was drenched with sweat and his clothes were filthy. The wood cut into his shoulder as he moved, following the prisoner who dragged himself painfully along before him.

Simon puzzled about the man. He could not see the prisoner's face, but it was clear that he had been barbarously scourged and had lost a great deal of blood. It was a mystery to Simon how the man had carried the cross as long as he did. Even he, Simon, vigorous and healthy as he was, could scarcely bear up under the burden.

What was the man's crime? What had he done to deserve crucifixion? He didn't seem a common criminal. Not once along the road had he opened his mouth to curse. Several times he had fallen, and the Roman soldier had kicked and beaten him back onto his feet, but there had never been an angry outburst or any reproach for the abuse heaped upon him.

Simon shook his head, uncomprehending. The man's feet were bare, and he left bloody footprints at each step. His garments were soaked with blood, and Simon knew that under the man's tunic his back was one raw wound. Dirt and animal dung from the street clung to his clothes. The cohort at the Praetorium had placed a crown of thorns on his head. His hair, which apparently had been a soft auburn, was now black and sticky with blood and pasted to his head. A green-bellied fly had settled on the back of the man's neck and was skittering back and forth.

The sight sickened Simon. The anger he had felt at having to carry the prisoner's cross drained from him, and his heart warmed toward the wretched man. In some strange, mysterious way he felt a bond of brotherhood with him.

Then — and Simon would always be hard pressed to explain what happened next — everything around him seemed to change. The rowdy mob ceased to mill about. In its stead marched a glorious pageant, men and women, chanting songs of victory. The strange man who walked before him no longer faltered but strode ahead, each moment growing in stature until he stood taller than any man should be, bigger, greater, and clothed in majestic splendor. The crown on his head had become a dazzling diadem, and above and about him myriads of voices were calling out, "Holy! Holy! Holy!"

Suddenly, Simon felt the sting of the lash, and someone was shouting.

"Drop it, fool!" It was the Roman.

Simon snapped to attention. For a moment he felt dazed, bewildered. When he came to his senses, he saw they were on the hilltop. The glory had faded, and the condemned man stood small in his helplessness. Simon let the cross go, and it slid from his shoulder to the ground with a heavy thud. At the sound, the prisoner turned and faced about. Simon looked at the man, then, stared in amazement. All the lost glory of a moment ago was there in the prisoner's eyes.

The End